UNIVERSITY OF
WOLVERHAMPTON

YOUNG RESEARCHER
THE AZTECS

Jacqueline Dineen

First published in 1992 by
Heinemann Children's Reference,
a division of Heinemann Educational Books Ltd,
Halley Court, Jordan Hill, Oxford OX2 8EJ.

OXFORD   LONDON   EDINBURGH
MADRID   PARIS   ATHENS   BOLOGNA
MELBOURNE   SYDNEY   AUCKLAND   SINGAPORE
TOKYO   IBADAN   NAIROBI   GABORONE   HARARE
PORTSMOUTH NH (USA)

Designed by Julian Holland Publishing Ltd
Picture Research by Ann-Marie Ehrlich
Colour artwork by Gecko and Martin Smillie
Editorial planning Jackie Gaff

Printed in Hong Kong

British Library Cataloguing in Publication Data

Dineen, Jacqueline
    The Aztecs. – (Young researcher)
    I. Title II. Series
    972.01

    ISBN 0-431-00568-0

92 93 94 95 96 11 10 9 8 7 6 5 4 3 2

Photographic acknowledgements

The authors and publishers wish to acknowledge with
thanks, the following photographic sources:
a = above b = below c = centre l = left r = right
Ferdinand Anton 20; Bodleian Library 10r, 11, 13b, 14-17, 28,
30a, 36, 42, 43b, 45, 46, 48; C. M. Dixon 7c, 33b; E. T. Archive
57; Werner Forman Archive 4, 5, 6l, 7b, 8l, 9, 10, 13, 18, 19, 20,
22, 23, 26, 27, 28, 29l, 31l, 32, 33a, 37, 39, 40, 47, 49, 53a, 59a;
Alan Hutchison Library 34, 35r; Mexican Embassy 59b;
Marion and Tony Morrison 44; Nick Saunders/Barbara
Heller Archive 6r; Salmer 54; Syndication International 24,
30b, 52r, 53.
The publishers have made every effort to trace the
copyright holders, but if they have inadvertently
overlooked any, they will be pleased to make the necessary
arrangement at the first opportunity.

Note to the reader
In this book there are some words in the text which are printed in **bold** type. This shows that the word is listed in the
glossary on page 62. The glossary gives a brief explanation of words which may be new to you.

Contents

Who were the Aztecs?

At the beginning of the sixteenth century, a great **civilization** flourished in the land that is now Mexico. The Aztec people, led by their lord Montezuma, ruled over a huge, rich **empire**. Their capital, Tenochtitlan, was one of the world's largest cities. In 1519 the Spanish attacked and destroyed the Aztec Empire, and destroyed a lot of the evidence that would have told us about how the Aztecs lived. Even so, there is enough left to give us an idea of their history.

Before the Aztecs

We know that civilizations existed in Mexico for about 2800 years before the Aztec Empire was finally destroyed. The first of these civilizations was the Olmecs who lived near the east coast from about 1300 BC. Olmec statues, carvings and ornaments that have been found show that they were skilled artists and **sculptors**.

The Maya civilization flourished between AD 300 and 900 on the Yucatan peninsula. The Maya were the first people in Mexico to use picture writing. Some of the books they produced still survive today.

The Toltecs were a warlike people who came from

△ **A Mixtec earring.** The Mixtec people arrived in Mexico in about 900. They were some of the most skilled crafts people in Mexico. The Aztecs copied some Mixtec styles so their jewellery looks similar. The Spaniards were after gold when they came to the Aztec capital city, Tenochtitlan, in 1519.

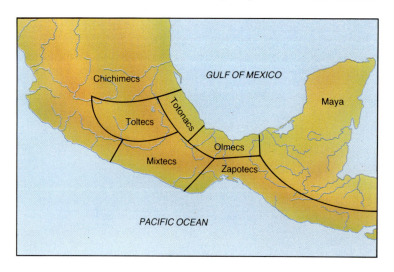

◁ **Some of the people who lived in Mexico before the Aztecs arrived**

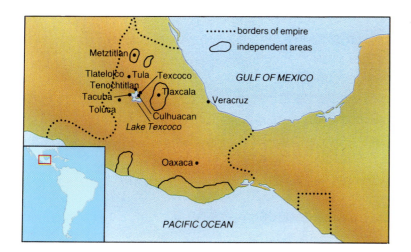

◁ **The Aztec empire in 1519**

the north and settled in the west of Mexico between 900 and 1150. Later on the Aztecs took over this area and they adopted some Toltec ideas. Ruins of buildings tell us that the Toltecs were great **architects**.

The Toltec empire began to lose power and its capital city, Tula, was destroyed in about 1150. Other tribes poured into the area. The last tribe to arrive was the Aztecs. They were a wandering tribe of hunters and farmers who called themselves the Mexica. A legend says that they left an island home, Aztlan, and travelled south because one of their gods told them to.

At first, the Aztecs had no land. They moved from place to place, trying to take land from other tribes. In about 1325 they settled on an island in the middle of Lake Texcoco and began to build their capital city Tenochtitlan. Today Mexico City stands on the site where Tenochtitlan once stood. Within 200 years, the Aztecs controlled an empire that stretched right across Mexico. Tenochtitlan became one of the biggest cities in the world. How did a poor tribe of farmers manage to build up such a mighty civilization in just 200 years?

△ **The Temple of the Warriors,** built by the Toltecs. In the background is a pyramid temple dedicated to the god Quetzalcoatl, the Feathered Serpent. The Aztecs turned the Toltecs into heroes who, they said, were wonderful artists and craftworkers. They also claimed the Toltecs were the ancestors of the Aztecs. When the Aztecs built their temples, they copied some of the details from Toltec temples.

5

Digging up the past

We know something about how the Aztecs lived from ruins of buildings, and remains of pottery, jewellery, and other **artefacts** which have been found. **Archaeologists** are people who piece together history from this sort of evidence. Often the evidence is buried deep in the earth, sometimes under modern buildings. Archaeologists might find out about the site of an ancient building by looking at old writings and maps. The archaeologists also **excavate** and uncover the ruins of buildings and towns. Often the buildings contain pots, coins, ornaments and other objects that people used in their everyday lives. Any evidence, however small, is collected together and examined.

Archaeology in Mexico

The Spaniards destroyed Tenochtitlan and later on Mexico City was built on top of the old capital. There is not much archaeological evidence about the city. Historians are still finding out about the Aztecs today. Sometimes new evidence is discovered by chance. A few years ago, a new underground station was being

△ **The excavated Templo Mayor** in Mexico City. This was the last Aztec temple to the gods Huitzilopochtli and Tlaloc. It stood in the square at the centre of Tenochtitlan. The archaeologists who excavated it found statues, vessels, and figures of gods and goddesses.

◁ **The remains of Teotihuacan.** Archaeologists and historians think the Aztecs copied the layout of Teotihuacan when they built their own city of Tenochtitlan. Teotihuacan covered 20 sq km. At its centre was a wide roadway lined with temples and palaces. There were two huge pyramid temples to the Sun and the Moon. The Aztecs also built a huge pyramid temple in the centre of Tenochtitlan. Both cities were divided into four quarters. The wealthy people lived nearest the centre, with farmers and craftworkers on the outskirts.

built in Mexico City. Archaeologists discovered an Aztec temple dedicated to Ehecatl-Quetzalcoatl, the God of the Wind. You can still see this pyramid temple today. Archaeologists have also excavated a large temple which was dedicated to the War God Huitzilopochtli and the Rain God Tlaloc. Artefacts such as statues give us clues about Aztec religion.

Archaeologists have been able to find out about other **civilizations** which influenced the Aztecs. They have uncovered the magnificent city of Teotihuacan which is about 50 kilometres from Mexico City. The city was built in about 200 BC but we do not know which tribes built it. It was destroyed in AD 750 and all its people moved away. First the Toltecs and then the Aztecs found it ruined and deserted. The Toltec capital city, Tula, has also been excavated. In Teotihuacan and Tula there are temples or carvings dedicated to Quetzalcoatl and Tlaloc, the same gods as the Aztecs worshipped. This tells us that the Aztecs borrowed some of their ideas from the Tula people. Teotihuacan, with its roads lined with temples and palaces, also seems to have given the Aztecs some ideas which they used when they built Tenochtitlan.

▽ **Aztec pottery.** The top picture shows a child's rattle which was made between 1300 and 1520. It is in the shape of a woman holding a child. The bottom picture shows small pottery stamps which the Aztecs used to print patterns in face paints onto their cheeks. Artefacts like these give us more clues about the Aztecs' way of life.

History in pictures and words

Most of what we know about the Aztecs comes from pictures and writings. Few of the Spaniards could understand the Aztecs' language. Priests came to Mexico to teach the people about Christianity. Some priests also tried to find out more about the Aztec **culture**. One of these was Father Bernadino de Sahagun who arrived in Mexico in 1529. He studied the Aztec language, Nahuatl, and talked to Aztec leaders.

Aztec writing

Sahagun tells us that the Aztecs did not have an alphabet but used picture symbols called **glyphs**. The glyphs were simple. A footprint meant travel, a scroll meant speech, a shield and arrows meant war.

The glyphs were painted onto a sort of paper called **amatl**, which was made from tree bark, or deer skin. The paper or skin was then folded like a concertina to make a book called a **codex**. The codices and other documents were written by **scribes** who used bright red, yellow, blue and green paints. The size and colour of the glyphs had a meaning. For example, important people were drawn larger than people who were less important, and colour was used to show rank.

The Spaniards burned most of the Aztec codices. They could not understand the glyphs and thought

△ **Aztec glyphs.** The glyphs are more like a code than the sort of writing we know. The scribes thought of pictures which described what they were trying to say. This glyph for the wind comes from the Codex Mendoza. It shows the Fire Serpent marrying a flower.

◁ **An example of an Aztec codex.** Picture symbols called glyphs were painted onto paper or deerskin which was folded into a book.

they were magic and evil. Sahagun's helpers, however, showed him some codices they had hidden. The glyphs were not like written sentences. They just helped to remind people what had happened, and the details of history and **legends** were passed on by word of mouth. Codices contained prayers, speeches, information about land and taxes, the calendar, and even information about the way children were brought up.

Sahagun persuaded his Aztec helpers to draw glyphs in answer to his questions about their history, religion and lifestyle before the Spanish came. When he had gathered his information, he wrote his great work, *General History of the Things of New Spain,* in Nahuatl and Spanish.

Other historians

Another Spanish historian of the time was Friar Diego Duran who produced a history in three books. In 1609 Don Fernando de Alvarado Tezozomoc, who was Montezuma's grandson, wrote his own history.

The problem with these histories is knowing what to believe. Sahagun and the other historians found that Aztec history was based on legends. For example, no one has ever been able to find the island that the Aztecs said they had come from. Also, the Aztecs probably liked to think their skills and achievements were greater than they actually were. On the other hand, the Spanish invaders tried to show the Aztecs as barbarians. People studying the evidence today have to remember who was writing and where their information came from.

Historians who write about the Aztecs today often call them the Mexica, the name they called themselves. They also spell Montezuma 'Moctezuma' which is a more accurate translation, although it is not so well known.

△ **A statue of the god Quetzalcoatl,** carrying grain on his back. The load is supported by a strap which passes round his forehead. This gives us an idea about how the Aztecs carried loads. Statues and ornaments tell us about clothing and appearance and also about materials used for craftworking. This statue was once covered in a type of plaster and painted.

Society and government

When the Aztecs first built Tenochtitlan, Mexico was divided into small **city-states**. Each city had its own ruler, the **tlatoani** (the Great Speaker). The Aztecs were aggressive people who wanted power. It was not long before they set out to conquer other city-states and build their **empire**. Each city-state that the Aztecs conquered had to pay **tributes** to them. These 'taxes' were paid in food and other goods. Tributes were collected by the *calipixque* or tax collectors.

The Aztecs were ruled by a king. The throne did not pass from father to son, although there was a royal family. When a king died, a group of **nobles**, priests and warriors chose the new ruler. The new ruler was always a brother of the dead king, or another

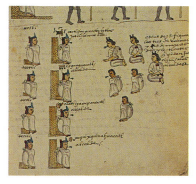

△ **Crime and punishment.** This picture from the Codex Mendoza shows an Aztec court trial. The six people on the right are seeking justice from the judges, who are shown on the left. Judges were chosen by the council. There was a main court in the city for nobles and serious cases, and smaller courts for the commoners. Punishments included piercing the prisoner with cactus spines, or taking his lands away. Thieves were stoned and sometimes hanged. Prisoners could appeal to the Woman Snake or the king if they did not agree with the findings of the trial.

◁ **The headdress of Montezuma,** king of the Aztecs, is made from precious stones and feathers from a tropical bird, the quetzal. The Aztec rulers built up their wealth as they conquered more lands. By the time the Spaniards arrived, the king lived in a magnificent palace and wore fine clothes and jewellery. He had a treasure house of gold. No one was allowed to look the king in the face. Even the nobles had to go barefoot in front of him.

member of his family.

The king had to keep tight control over the empire. This often led to war, so he had to be a good soldier. The most important person after the king was called the Woman Snake, though he was actually a man. He controlled law and order and the collection of taxes. There was also a **council** of four nobles. Land in the Aztec empire was divided up between a group of powerful noblemen, who also owned the other valuable resources such as gold mines.

Sahagun wrote in his history of the Aztecs that if an Aztec man was to be a noble, he had to be able to trace his family back to the first Aztec ruler. The noblemen chose the council from among their own group. There was also a larger council called the *tlatocan,* which included tax collectors, judges and scribes.

The calpulli family group

Every Aztec was a member of a **calpulli**. This was a clan or group of families who were related to each other. Towns and villages were organized around the calpullis that lived in them. The calpullis owned land but were under the strict control of the king and the nobles. The land was farmed on a **communal** basis. It belonged to everyone and the **peasants** or ordinary working people were not allowed to own their own plot. Each calpulli had to send tributes to the ruler and nobility.

Each calpulli had a **calpullec** or head man. He was chosen by the people and took his orders from the nobles. He had to divide up the calpulli's land and look after it, make sure its tributes were paid and provide workers for the nobles. The nobles quickly became more powerful as the Aztecs built up their empire after the 1420s. They dominated the calpullis more and more.

△ **A tribute list** was a list of what the people of a city-state had to pay to the Aztecs if the Aztecs had conquered them. This tribute list from the Codex Mendoza shows the tribute paid by 22 towns in an area called Tochtepec. Every year these towns had to send: *1600 rich mantles, 800 striped red, white and green mantles, 400 warriors' tunics and shirts. One war dress with 'bird device' as shown. Gold headbands, beads, also jadeite, amber labrets (lip plugs). 800 bundles of rich green quetzal feathers. 8000 little bundles of rich blue feathers. 8000 little bundles of rich red feathers. 8000 little bundles of rich green feathers. 200 loads of cocoa, 16 000 balls of oli which is the gum of trees, and these balls when thrown on the ground bounce very high...*

The clothes the Aztecs wore

The Aztecs thought it was important to know what a person's position in society was, whether high or low. People's rank showed in the way they dressed. There were three main groups, the **nobility**, the **commoners** and the **slaves**. Commoners were the ordinary farmers, fishermen and craftsmen. They all had to pay tributes to the nobles, either by working for them or by making the goods the nobles needed. Duran writes about slavery in his history. People who could not pay their tributes or who were too poor to live off the land sometimes chose to be slaves. Commoners could become slaves by selling themselves at a slave market. The people who bought the slaves were expected to feed and clothe them.

The rules of dress

Only the nobility were allowed to wear sandals in the city, and to wear **capes** made of cotton. The commoners had to wear coarse cloth made from **maguey** cactus or palm fibres. They could not wear clothes that reached beneath their knees. A commoner who wore a robe to the ankles was killed.

◁ **Aztec clothes,** from the Florentine Codex. The man on the right is obviously a nobleman. He wears a decorated cloak knotted on the shoulder and reaching below his knees. He also wears sandals. The woman on the left wears a length of cloth knotted at the waist to make a skirt. She also wears a cape and sandals. The cloth is dyed in bright colours.

◁ **Gold nose and ear plugs** were worn by Aztec men and women. Men and women also pierced their ears and wore earrings. Men pierced the lower lip to wear lip plugs. You could only wear the jewellery of your social rank. Only the king and lords could wear gold armbands and anklets, and gold rattles on their feet.

The Aztecs grew cotton and maguey plants and spun fibres into thread. Lengths of cloth were woven on simple **looms**. Every Aztec woman was expected to weave. Most Aztec clothes were simply lengths of cloth worn as they came off the loom. The cloth could be knotted over the shoulders as a cloak or wrapped round the body to make a woman's skirt. Every male wore a **loin cloth**.

The most important garment was the rectangular cape. The **embroidery** and decoration on the cape showed what position the wearer held in life. Capes could be awarded for bravery in battle. The Codex Mendoza tells how warriors who captured two prisoners were awarded a cape with an orange border. Capes were given as tributes and used for trading.

The Aztecs liked bright colours and dyed their cloth with natural dyes made from flowers, vegetables, shellfish or insects. For example, the **cochineal** insect provided a brilliant red dye.

△ **Learning to weave.** This glyph from the Codex Mendoza shows a woman teaching her daughter to weave. The girl is using a simple loom, called a backstrap loom. The picture also shows the clothes and hairstyles of the mother and daughter. No Aztec cloth or clothing survives, even though Mexico is a fairly dry country. All of the old cloth has rotted away. So we have to rely on glyphs like these and a few wall paintings to tell us what the Aztecs wore.

Family life

Each Aztec family was closely connected to its **calpulli**, as the calpulli owned land and gave it to the families to grow food on. We know something about the calpulli land from the writings of the Spanish judge, Alonso de Zorita, in 1585. When a man and woman got married, they were given a plot of land to work. They could ask the **calpullec** for more land when they had children and needed to grow more food. The land could only be taken away if the family did not farm it properly. Each family had to work for the calpullec and give him some of their produce in payment for the work he did.

Marriage

The Aztecs always married someone in their own social class. Marriages were arranged. A boy was

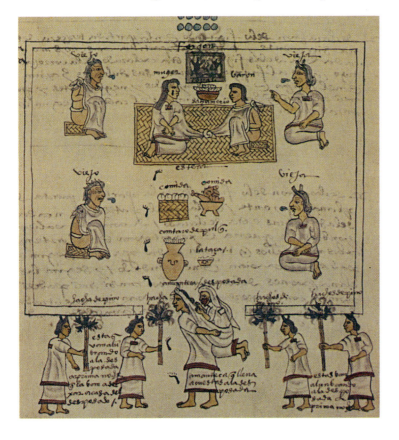

◁ **An Aztec wedding,** from the Codex Mendoza. On the day of the marriage, the guests arrived and feasted all day long. In the evening, the bride was dressed in red feathers and her face was painted red. The bridegroom's relatives lectured her about being a good wife. Then they carried her to the bridegroom's house in a torchlit procession. This is shown at the bottom of the picture. The top part of the picture shows the bride and bridegroom sitting together on mats in front of the hearth. Their cloaks have been tied together to show that they are now tied as man and wife. After the ceremony, the couple were left alone in the bridegroom's house for four days. On the fifth day, there was another ceremony and feast when the two families lectured the couple about married life.

14

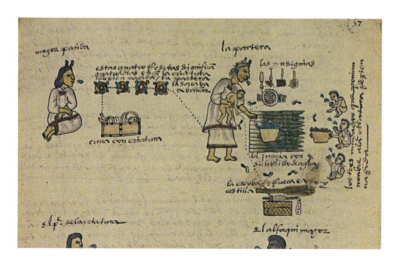

◁ **The first days in a baby's life,** from the Codex Mendoza. The picture on the left shows a mother lecturing her new-born baby. As soon as babies were born, they were taught that they had to work hard. The four rosettes above the cradle show that this baby is four days old. A midwife helped with the birth. On a lucky day chosen by the soothsayer, the child was bathed and named. The picture on the right shows the midwife taking the baby to be washed.

thought to be ready for marriage as soon as he left school at 20. His father arranged a feast and found a suitable teenage girl. A **matchmaker** was brought in to settle the details between the two families. It does not seem that the boy and girl had any say in all this. The matchmaker settled the bride's **dowry**, the gift of land or goods that the bride's father would give the husband. Then the families went to a **soothsayer** for advice on the wedding date.

Noblemen were allowed more than one wife. Rulers and nobles usually made marriages that increased their land or possessions, by marrying a woman whose father could provide a good dowry. It seems that commoners only had one wife, but this may have been because they could not afford any more.

Babies

Birth dates were important to the Aztecs. As soon as a baby was born, the parents went to the soothsayer who told them the baby's fate, based on its birth date. The soothsayer also advised on a good day for the naming of the child. They believed that a person's character was affected by his or her birth date.

Children's toys
The toys that Aztec children played with prepared them for what was expected of them as men or women when they grew up. A boy was expected to follow his father's craft or trade and also to be a brave warrior. His parents gave him a tiny shield, a bow and arrows, a **cape** and **loincloth**, and the tools of his father's craft or trade. A girl was expected to stay at home, weaving and working in the house. She was given a tiny spindle for spinning thread, and a broom.

Growing up and going to school

Children had to help with household work, such as carrying water and firewood, from the age of four or five. Older children helped with farming and fishing. If the parents were craftworkers, the children began to learn about their parents' craft. We know from the codices that parents often gave their children lectures, telling them that hard work was the key to success in life.

The sons of nobles were brought up in a way that prepared them for life as soldiers and speakers. Girls all stayed at home and learned to spin, weave, cook and clean.

A boy's education

Boys from noble families went to a temple school, the **calmecac**, when they were 12. They stayed till they were 15. The school concentrated on military training but the boys also learned about the law, the calendar, Aztec customs and religion, and the famous speeches of the past. Only a few people could understand the codices so the boys had to learn all this information off by heart. The schools were very strict. Teachers would jab boys with a cactus spine for misbehaving. If a boy did something very bad he was shot with arrows!

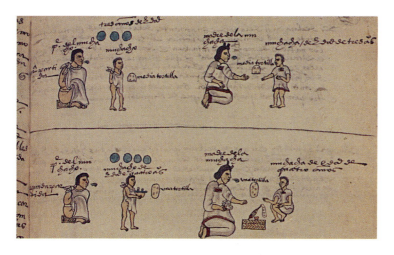

◁ **Aztec parents teaching young children.** The pictures on the left show a father with boys aged between three and six (the blue dots show how old each child is). On the right, a mother teaches girls of the same ages. Small boys carried loads for their fathers. Small girls learned to spin. The yellow shapes show how many tortillas the children were allowed each day.

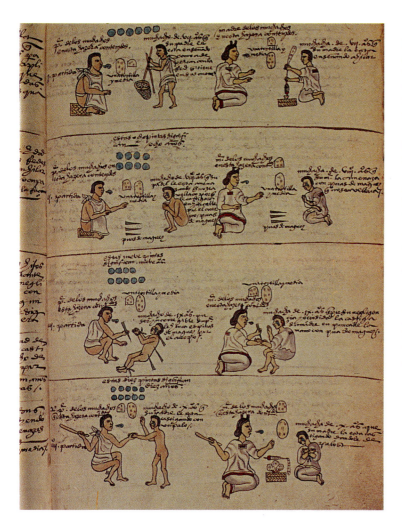

◁ **Parents teaching and punishing older children.** The pictures show fathers and boys on the left, and mothers and girls on the right. At the top, a father teaches his son to fish. In the second picture, a boy is warned that he will be punished if he tells lies. The third picture shows a boy being pricked with cactus spines. In the bottom picture, a boy is beaten with a stick. These were typical punishments for older children. At the top right, a girl is taught to spin by her mother. The three lower pictures show girls receiving similar punishments to the boys. The Aztecs were strict parents who taught their children that they must behave well and follow the Aztec rules for a good life.

The sons of commoners went to a **telpocticalli** when they reached their teens. This was a school run by their **calpulli**. The boys lived at the school. They learned to use weapons because every young man was expected to fight in wars. They also had some religious teaching and worked in the fields.

Boys and girls went to a **cuicalli** (House of Song) between the ages of 12 and 15. Here they learnt the songs, dances and music that went with the Aztec religion. For the girls, this was the only education they had outside the home.

What the Aztecs believed

The Aztecs worshipped many different gods but they believed that they had been specially chosen by the Sun God, Huitzilopochtli. The Aztecs had a legend about how they came to Mexico. The legend says that they left the island of Aztlan because the priests told them that the god would make them 'lords and kings of all that is in the world'. In fact, historians think that the Sun God was not really as important to the earlier tribes as the Aztecs liked to think. The first Woman Snake, Tlalacel, made the people believe that they were specially chosen so that they would be more warlike and aggressive.

The Aztecs believed that the gods controlled everything in their lives and everything that grew on Earth. The Aztecs felt they must keep the gods happy, so almost everything that happened had some religious ceremony to go with it.

Life after death

The Aztecs believed in an afterlife. What kind of afterlife you had depended on what you had been in life. For example, a brave soldier who was killed in battle travelled round with the sun for four years and then returned to Earth as a hummingbird. Women who died in childbirth were thought to become like goddesses after death.

When people died, their families would dress the bodies up in their finest clothes. The families and friends danced and chanted funeral prayers for four days. Then the dead were **cremated**. Their ashes were buried with their best possessions and enough food for the journey to the **underworld**. The Aztecs believed that this journey took them past high mountains and across eight deserts. On the way they had to fight snakes and lizards and tackle other hardships. Their success depended on how wealthy and how well behaved they had been in life.

△ **Some of the gods the Aztecs worshipped.** Every family had these household statues and everything the Aztecs did was bound up in religion. They believed that the gods, and particularly Huitzilopochtli, had to be fed with human blood and hearts each day. When they set off into battle, one purpose was to capture as many prisoners as possible. These were killed in the temples and offered to Huitzilopochtli. In some ceremonies, thousands of prisoners were killed at a time.

THE AZTEC GODS

The Aztecs believed that the gods lived above the earth, in 13 layers of heaven. The most powerful gods lived in the top layers. The most important god was called Huitzilopochtli. He was the Sun God, and also the God of War. The Aztecs believed that there was a constant struggle between good and evil. The sun was good but, when evil won, the sun was destroyed. They believed that four suns had been created and destroyed before and that the gods were the fifth sun. If they did not please the gods, the fifth sun would go out and the world would be plunged into darkness. That is why they had to worship the Sun God. They did this by killing people and offering their blood to the sun. They believed that the sun needed a constant supply of human blood to give it strength and keep it moving across the sky.

The legend of Quetzalcoatl

Quetzalcoatl, the Feathered or Plumed Serpent, was the god who looked after learning and schools. He was also the god who created new life and, using the name Ehecatl-Quetzalcoatl, he was the God of the Wind. He also made the soil rich. The Aztecs had several different legends about Quetzalcoatl. One legend says that he founded the Toltec city of Tula. He took on human form as a priest and ruled over Tula. There was a power struggle between Quetzalcoatl and the Toltec war god, Tezcatlipoca. Quetzalcoatl fled to the east coast. The story goes that he made a raft of serpents and set off across the sea, saying that he would return to claim back his lands. In pictures and statues Quetzalcoatl usually wears a bird-like mask and a feathered headdress.

Other gods

It was difficult for the Aztecs to grow crops because there was so little rain. Many religious ceremonies involved praying for rain and successful crops. Tlaloc was the God of Rain and his wife, Chalchihuitlicue, was a water goddess. Maize was the main crop and formed the basis of Aztec meals. Chicomecoatl, or Xilonen, was the goddess of the young maize plants. Another goddess, Ometochtli, watched over the maguey cactus. Tetesinnan was known as the Mother of the Gods, or earth mother. She was the goddess of childbirth. Xipe Totec was the God of Planting and Spring. Xiuhtecutli was the oldest of the gods. He was the God of Fire, who gave all living things the warmth they needed.

A mask of Quetzalcoatl decorated with turquoise.

A mask of the goddess Chalchihuitlicue.

Festivals and temples

The Aztecs had at least 18 important religious ceremonies a year. Most of these were to do with the farming year. Many of them gave prayers or thanks to the rain god, Tlaloc, and to the goddesses of water, maize and the land.

There were also smaller ceremonies. The Aztecs believed that they had to offer the blood of some creature to the sun each day, otherwise the sun would not rise. The priests offered the blood of a bird, the quail. The historian Sahagun writes 'Each day, when the sun arose, quails were slain... they raised them, dedicated them to the sun'. People who wanted forgiveness from the gods pricked their bodies with a cactus spine to draw blood. The priests also **sacrificed** animals and people to keep the gods happy. Human blood was the most precious offering of all. The sacrifice of people to the sun was an important part of Aztec religion. If the Aztecs really wanted to please the gods at an important ceremony such as the planting of the maize crop, they sacrificed people in costumes that represented the gods themselves. Aztec priests sacrificed people by stabbing them. After prisoners had been sacrificed there was a feast where the warriors and the priests ate the victims' flesh. This is called **cannibalism**.

Some festivals did not take place every year. Sahagun writes about a festival which took place every eight years and gave new life to the maize. Everyone dressed up as butterflies, hummingbirds and other animals and danced to the rain god, Tlaloc.

Celebrating the new age
The largest festival of all took place every 52 years. The Aztecs believed that every 52 years one age ended and a new one began. Everyone cleaned their houses and threw away their cooking pots and statues of the gods. At midnight a person was

△ **A boy offering a melon to the gods.** Boys were encouraged from childhood to become priests. There were thousands of priests in the temples. They could be commoners or nobles. They could work their way up to be chief priests. Priests taught in the schools, organized religious ceremonies, kept the fires burning in the temple and of course sacrificed offerings to the gods. Their clothes were blood-spattered. They painted their faces black and their hair was long and matted because they never cut, washed or combed it. Some women became priestesses.

sacrificed on top of a holy hill near the city and a fire was lit over the body. This was the 'new fire' of the next 52 years. Torches were lit from the new fire and people ran with the torches to the temples, schools and houses. They believed that the world would end if they did not carry out this ceremony.

The temples

There were many temples in every city. The temples were solid mounds of earth covered in mud bricks or stone. Everything happened on the outside of the temple so that everyone could see it. The temples were built as high as possible so that the priests were nearer to the gods. The temples were in the shape of a pyramid and had flights of steps up the outside. There were galleries round the building at different levels. At the top of the temple was a large flat area. This was the place where sacrifices were made. Here, there were one or two towers containing statues of the god or gods the temple was for. There were altars where fires were always kept burning.

▽ **The great temple and square in Tenochtitlan** probably looked like this, according to descriptions given by the Spaniards and evidence found by archaeologists. The temple was 150 m high and took up most of the north side of the square. You can see the two small chapels to the gods on the top. Huitzilopochtli's was red and Tlaloc's was blue. The rooftops were decorated with shells. The walls of the temple were covered in a type of plaster and decorated with sculptures and paintings in bright colours. Two steep flights of 114 steps led up to the top of the pyramid. Here, there was a drum which could be heard about 10 km away.

The Aztec calendar

An accurate calendar was important to the Aztecs. They had to know when to hold their religious festivals. They had to be able to work out the years in which various things would happen, particularly the end of each 52 years, when they believed that a new age began.

In fact, the Aztecs had two separate calendars. The **solar** calendar was based on the movement of the sun round the Earth. This calendar marked the seasons and the times for planting and harvesting the crops. It was based on the earlier Maya calendar. The Maya people had found a system of using numbers which is very similar to the numbering we use today. They had worked out that there were 365.242 days in a year. The Aztecs based their calendar on the number 20, the number of fingers and toes a person has. They divided the year into months of 20 days. 18 months made up a year of 360 days. This left five days over. The Aztecs were afraid of these days because they had no gods watching over them. They thought of

◁ **The Aztec Calendar Stone** or Stone of the Sun was ordered to be made in the 1470s by the ruler Axayacatl. After the Spaniards came, the stone was lost for more than 200 years until it was dug up by accident in 1790. It was found under the great square in Mexico City and is now in the Aztec gallery in Mexico's National Museum of Anthropology. The stone weighs 24 tonnes. In the centre is the Sun God. The four squares around him show the four suns that the Aztecs believed existed before their own sun. In the other rings are the day names, signs showing precious things, the sun's ray, star signs, and two snakes which are symbols of time.

◁ **A carving showing the 'tying up of the years'.** This happened at the end of every 52 years when, the Aztecs believed, one age ended and a new one began. Each 52-year period was called 'a bundle of years'. The priests kept count by putting aside a peeled reed for each year. When they had collected 52 reeds, they tied them together and buried them. This meant it was time to start a new bundle of years with a new fire ceremony.

them as evil days when bad things could happen.

The sacred or holy calendar was only used for religious festivals. It had 260 days in a year, divided into four groups of 65 days. Each group was divided into five 'weeks' of 13 days. This calendar was known as the **tonalpohualli**, the 'Count of Days'. Each day in the year had a different meaning. This was worked out by linking each of the 20 'day signs' with each of the numbers between 1 and 13 days. Each day sign was shown by a glyph.

Reading the calendar

Certain days on the sacred calendar were lucky or unlucky. Only priests who had studied **astrology** could read the lucky and unlucky days. Astrology is the study of how the stars affect people's lives. The Aztecs believed that the Earth was a flat disc surrounded by a ring of water. Above the disc were the heavens which had 13 layers. Each layer had its own gods, and each god ruled over different days of the sacred calendar.

People always visited an astrologer for advice before doing anything important. The astrologers chose lucky days for the naming ceremony for new babies, and used people's birth dates to tell them what their future would be.

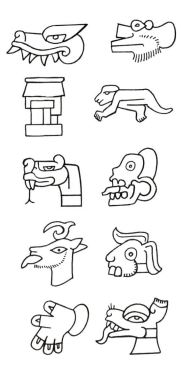

△ **The Count of Days.** Each day from 1 to 20 had a glyph to describe it. Here are some examples.

1 crocodile	2 wind
3 house	4 lizard
5 snake	6 death
7 deer	8 rabbit
9 water	10 dog

The lake city of Tenochtitlan

The city of Tenochtitlan began on an island in the middle of a swampy lake. There the Aztecs built their first temple to Huitzilopochtli. The place was given the name Tenochtitlan, which means 'The Place of the Fruit of the Prickly Pear Cactus'. Later on the name was given to the city that grew up around the temple. The Aztecs rebuilt their temples on the same site every 52 years, so the first temple eventually became the great Templo Mayor that stood at the centre of the city.

The city started as a collection of huts. It began to grow after 1385, while Acamapichtli was king. The Aztecs were excellent engineers. They built three **causeways** over the swamp to link the city with the mainland. These were raised roads made of stone supported on wooden pillars. The causeways had bridges over them. These bridges could be removed to leave gaps and this prevented enemies getting to the city. Fresh water was brought from the mainland to the city along stone **aqueducts**.

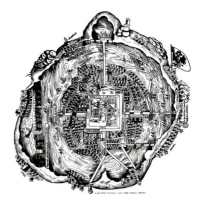

△ **Cortes's map of Tenochtitlan** gives us some idea of the city layout. You can see the main square in the middle, with the temple on one side of it. The king's palace was on the other side of the square. Nearby, there were smaller temples. For example there were temples to Quetzalcoatl, Tezcatlipoca and Coatlicue, the mother of Huitzilopochtli.

Inside the city

The Spaniards' first view of Tenochtitlan was described by one of Cortes's soldiers, Bernal Diaz, 'And when we saw all those towns and villages built in the water...and that straight and level causeway leading into Mexico, we were astounded. These great towns...and buildings rising from the water, all made of stone, seemed like an enchanted vision.'

By that time Tenochtitlan was the largest city in Mexico. About 200 000 people lived there. The houses were one storey high and had flat roofs. In the centre of the city was a large square. The temple stood on one side, and the king's palace on another. Officials' houses made of white stone also lined the square. There were few roads. People travelled in canoes along canals.

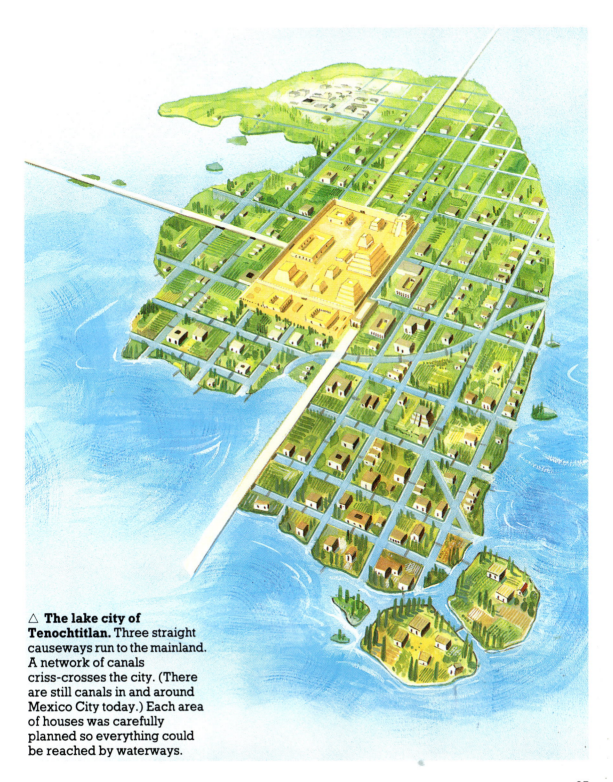

△ **The lake city of
Tenochtitlan.** Three straight
causeways run to the mainland.
A network of canals
criss-crosses the city. (There
are still canals in and around
Mexico City today.) Each area
of houses was carefully
planned so everything could
be reached by waterways.

Floating gardens

Tenochtitlan was built in a huge valley, the Valley of Mexico, which was surrounded by mountains. Rivers flowed from the mountains into Lake Texcoco, where Tenochtitlan stood. The lake was linked to four other shallow swampy lakes. The land around the lakes was dry because there was very little rain.

The Aztecs drained parts of the lake to make thousands of **chinampas** or swamp gardens which could be farmed. The gardens were linked by drainage **dykes** or ditches which carried water into larger canals. The dykes and canals were used for **irrigation** and as waterways to the city.

Texcoco and the lake to the south contained fresh water, but the northern lakes contained salt water which was no good for irrigation. The Aztecs built an embankment 16 kilometres long to keep out the salt water and also to protect the city from flooding.

Feeding the people

Archaeologists think that when Tenochtitlan was at its greatest, about a million people lived in the Valley of Mexico. That included Tenochtitlan and the 50 or 60 **city-states** on the mainland surrounding the lakes. Food for all these people had to come from farming.

◁ **The maguey cactus plant** had many uses. Parts of it were made into medicines. Open wounds were dressed with maguey pulp and salt. The thorns were used as needles for sewing. People who had done wrong were pricked with maguey thorns. The fibres were spun together and then woven into a coarse cloth. The flesh of the plant was made into a popular drink, *pulque.* The maguey had its own goddess, Mayahuel. In this picture maguey cactus plants are growing in front of a reconstructed Aztec temple.

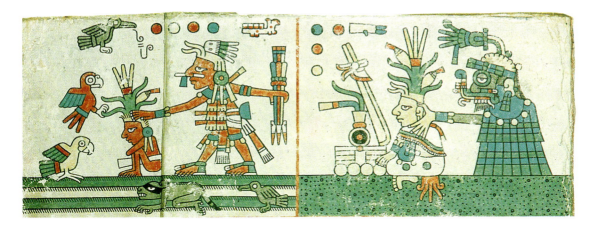

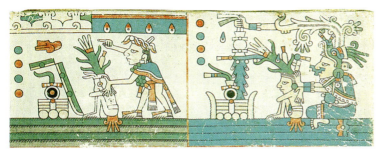

Historians are not sure how many people in Tenochtitlan were farmers, but they think it may have been between half and one third of the population. The rest were the nobility, craftsmen and others. Each chinampa was only big enough to grow food for one family. Most people in Tenochtitlan depended on food from outside the city.

As the city grew, more and more land was drained for farming and for building on. Farmers had no tools except simple hoes and digging sticks but the loose soil was **fertile** and easy to turn. The main crop was maize, but farmers also grew tomatoes, beans, chilli peppers and prickly pears. They grew maguey cactus for its fibres and to make a drink called **pulque**. Cocoa trees were grown in the hottest areas. The beans were used for trading and to make a chocolate drink.

△ **The life of a maize plant over four years,** from an Aztec codex. Over half the farmland was taken up with growing maize. Even so, there was hardly enough to go round. If a crop failed, people starved. Maize was so important to the Aztecs that special gods and goddesses were in charge of it. On the right of the first picture, Tlaloc, the God of Rain, pours water on to the plant. The plant is shown as Chalchihuitlicue, Tlaloc's wife, with strong roots in wet soil. In the second year, on the left, there is very little rain. Xipe Totec, the god of planting and spring, is in charge of the maize. The earth is dry and the plant cannot take root. It is attacked by birds and animals. In the third year, on the right of the second picture, the storm goddess pours water onto a strong young plant. The fourth year, on the left, is bad again. The plant is wilting and the soil is so dry that the digging stick in front of the plant is broken.

Inside an Aztec home

There were big differences between a rich Aztec home and a poor one. The **nobles'** houses were like palaces. They were one storey high and built round a courtyard. Each of the four sides contained four or five large rooms. The courtyards were planted with flower and vegetable gardens. Some houses on the island in the centre of the city were built of **adobe** – bricks made from mud and dried in the sun. Adobe is still used for building in Mexico today. These grand houses and palaces were whitewashed so that they shone in the sun. The Spanish soldier Bernal Diaz described buildings that looked like 'gleaming white towers and castles: a marvellous sight'.

There is very little evidence about the buildings in Tenochtitlan and hardly any about the poor people's houses. What we do know has been pieced together from scattered historical records such as documents that record the sale of building sites on the **chinampa** gardens. All of the poorer people's homes were built on the chinampas on the outskirts of the city. Because the chinampas would not take the weight of stone, houses had to be built of lighter materials such as wattle-and-daub. This was made by weaving reeds together and then plastering them with mud. We know that the outskirts of the city were divided into groups of houses inside walled areas or **compounds**. A whole family lived in each compound. The family consisted of a couple, their married children and their grandchildren. Every married couple in the family had a separate house of one or two rooms. All the houses opened onto an outdoor patio which belonged to the whole family.

Outside the house, the families often kept turkeys in pens. The turkeys provided eggs and meat. There was also a beehive for honey. Most families had a bath-house in the garden.

△ **The king's palace.** This drawing from the Codex Mendoza gives us some idea of what Montezuma's palace looked like. It was almost like a small town. There was the main palace with older palaces round about. The buildings had two storeys. The king lived on the upper floor of the main palace. You can see him in the central room. On the ground floor were council offices, law courts and store rooms for tributes. City leaders came to the palace each day to get their orders from the king. The buildings were divided by courtyards and gardens, and there were cages of wild animals and birds. The walls of the palace were decorated with carvings, and brightly coloured paintings.

Furniture and decoration

Aztec houses were very bare inside. Everyone slept on mats of reeds which were spread on the earth floor at night. Families had cooking pots and utensils made of clay. There were goblets for **pulque** and other drinks, graters for grinding chillis, and storage pots of various designs. Reed baskets were also used for storage. Households had grinding stones for grinding maize into flour. There was also a household **shrine** with statues of the gods.

The houses had no windows or chimneys so they must have been dark and smoky from the cooking fire. There were no doors, just an open doorway. Even the palaces had open doorways with cloths hanging over them.

△ **Inside an Aztec house.** This picture from the Florentine Codex shows an Aztec home just after the new fire of another 52-year age has been brought in. The new fire burns in the hearth, which was sacred to the Aztecs. There is no furniture and the man and woman sit on a reed mat. A girl is cooking over a fire at the front of the picture.

◁ **This priest's house at Teotihuacan** is probably similar to the homes of Aztec nobles. You can see the doorways opening onto a central courtyard. The outside walls are decorated with carvings and it has stone floors. The flat roofs of the houses often had flower gardens on them.

Cooking and eating

Aztec women were expected to concentrate on household work. Noblewomen had to be good cooks so that they could organize their servants. The wives of commoners spent their lives cooking, weaving and looking after their children. Aztec women cooked the family's food over a hearth, which was the centre of the home. Three stones were arranged in a triangle and a flat stone was laid over the top for the cooking pots to rest on.

Everyday food

The Aztecs cooked by boiling, grilling or roasting. Food was never fried. Maize was the main food. Every day, the women ground it into flour and made **tortillas**. The flour was mixed with water and shaped into flat pancakes. The tortillas were laid over the stone on the fire to cook. Maize was also made into a sort of porridge or gruel called **atolli**. There were several recipes. One writer who knew the Aztecs listed 'maize gruel with honey, with chilli and honey, with yellow chilli' and 'white, thick gruel with a scattering of maize grains'. The Aztecs also made maize pancakes called **tamales**. The same writer describes 'white tamales with beans, forming a sea shell on top' and 'tamales made of maize flowers with ground amaranth seed and cherries added'.

There was very little meat so the Aztecs had to eat other foods for **protein**. Beans appeared in many meals. They were boiled and flavoured with tomato and chilli. A flower called amaranth provided flavouring for many dishes. Amaranth seeds were made into **pinole**, which was a type of thin porridge. Other flowers were also used to add flavour to food. Most dishes were flavoured with chilli.

Turkeys and dogs were the only animals that the Aztecs kept. People had to hunt for any other meat. They trapped rabbits and deer and netted the wild

△ **Grinding maize.** In the top picture from the Codex Mendoza, a mother teaches her daughter how to grind maize to make flour. The girl uses a roller made of stone called a *metate* to crush the grains. The *metate* was rolled up and down a block of stone called a *mano*. It was hard, slow work to make enough flour for the day's tortillas and tamales. Maize is still ground in this way in parts of Mexico. The Aztecs stored grain in pots like the ones in the bottom picture.

◁ **These bowls were used for preparing food.** There are scratch marks on the inside which show that the bowls were probably used for grinding peppers. The Aztecs did not have pottery wheels so they shaped the pots by hand and then painted them. These pots were made by coiling strips of clay. Archaeologists have found examples of Aztec pottery. Pottery roasting dishes were used for cooking tortillas over the fire. There were no knives and forks. People ate with their fingers but rich families had serving spoons made of metals.

ducks that flew over the lakes. The lakes were full of fish, although the Aztecs do not seem to have been great fishermen. One writer tells us that they caught turtles, salamanders, frogs and shellfish from the lakes. The Aztecs also gathered wild fruit and vegetables such as figs and nuts to add to their meals.

Food for the nobility

Most of what the hunters caught went to feed the Aztec nobility. Their food included birds like quail, pigeons, geese, pelicans and cranes. Roast turkey was a favourite dish. Most people drank **pulque** but a favourite drink with the nobles was **chocolatl** which was made from cocoa beans. This is where our word 'chocolate' comes from but it was nothing like the sweets you buy today. The cocoa beans were crushed and made into a frothy drink flavoured with **vanilla** and spices. Beans, chillis, turkey, fruit and vegetables are still the main ingredients of the Mexican diet today.

△ **A hairless dog.** Aztec families kept dogs as pets but they also kept a special breed of hairless dog for the table. Young puppies were roasted and eaten on special occasions and at feasts and banquets. These pottery models show what the hairless dogs looked like.

Feasts and entertainment

The rich nobles in Tenochtitlan often held large banquets. There were many servants to serve food to the guests. The house was scented with perfumes and herbs and flowers were thrown around as the guests arrived. Each guest was given water and a cotton napkin. They ate with their fingers but they were expected to wash their hands before and after the meal. When they had washed, the men smoked tobacco in pipes or cigars. They pressed their nostrils together with their fingers to suck in the smoke. They also crushed dried tobacco leaves to make **snuff** which they breathed in through their noses. The women joined these banquets but sat apart from the men. We do not know if they were allowed to smoke.

Food for the king

The feast would be enormous with a huge choice of dishes. Some people have said that King Montezuma could choose from 100 different dishes every day. There would be many different kinds of roast meats, mainly birds and a special delicacy, roast dog. These meats were served with different sauces, and every sort of vegetable and fruit that grew in the area. There would also be pastries made from maize flour and sugar. The Aztecs knew how to make sugar from maize stalks.

The table would be decorated with silver or gold vases. Drinking cups and spoons were made of gold, silver or tortoise shell. Everyone, even the king, ate with their fingers.

After the meal, the young people got up to dance. An orchestra played drums, rattles, flutes, whistles and trumpets made of shell. Statues have been found which show what some of these instruments looked like. The other guests sat around the table drinking **pulque** and talking.

△ **The Aztecs were graceful dancers.** This pottery figure is probably of a trained dancer and singer. He is singing a song, perhaps in praise of the king. This figure tells us a lot about the dancers. You can see that he is wearing a loin-cloth, which he is holding with one hand. He also has a lip-plug and earrings.

Ceremonies and festivals

Ceremonies and festivals for the gods always included singing and dancing. Professional singers and dancers were trained at the **calmecac**. They learned to compose and sing songs about the gods and wonderful deeds of the rulers. The Aztecs thought highly of these singers and dancers. Each temple had a **tlapizcatzin** or caretaker who trained the singers.

Most festivals ended with feasting and merry-making. Sometimes the king and the nobles paid for the feast and all the city's people took part.

△ **A** *teponaztli* **or two-tone drum** provided the rhythm for the dancing. The outside of this one is made of carved wood. The carving shows the head of a bird. It could be an owl or an eagle. This type of drum had two flaps of wood on top that produced different musical notes when the drummer hit them.

◁ **A pottery whistle.** Musicians played small whistles like this to mark time for the dancers. On the top of the whistle is a stamp with a monkey pattern on it. Musicians also played pottery flutes and another wind instrument called an ocarina. Rattles were made from the shells of gourds, which are a kind of fruit.

Sports and games

Nobles and commoners enjoyed playing the sacred ball game **tlachtli**. They played it on important festival days, and also to settle bets and just to entertain themselves and the crowd that was watching the game.

Hundreds of people came to watch big matches. They placed bets on who they thought would win. The bets could involve anything from precious stones to slaves, and even people's houses and land.

The modern games of netball and basketball are based on tlachtli. Tlachtli was played on a special court with a line across the middle. There were two rings on each side of the line.

The players were specially trained. The game was played very fast with a hard rubber ball, so the players wore protective clothing such as gloves and

▽ **This tlachtli court** at Chichen Itza, on the Yucatan peninsula, was built by the Toltecs, who took over the area from the Maya people. The Mayas played tlachtli before the Toltecs, and later the Aztecs discovered it. Tlachtli was played with a ball made from the sap of rubber trees, which grow wild in the rain forests of South America.

hip-guards made of deerskin. The idea was to hit the ball backwards and forwards with the hip or the knee. Players were not allowed to hit the ball with any other part of the body. Goals were scored by getting the ball through one of the two rings. If a player managed to get the ball through a ring, his team won the game. The winners were allowed to confiscate possessions from any of the spectators they could catch.

Gambling

Everyone played a dice game called **patolli**. The dice were white beans. Players threw the beans and moved pebbles around a board. There were patolli tournaments where gamblers bet heavily. One Spanish writer tells us how people ended up gambling their homes, their fields, their corn granaries and their cactus plants.

△ **The volador ceremony** in Mexico today is similar to the Aztec volador ceremony. This was a spectacular religious occasion where men tried to imitate the flight of the gods. Four men were attached to a central pole by ropes. The men circled round as the ropes unwound. Each man went round the pole 13 times, which was the number of days in the week.

63.

◁ **A patolli game,** from the Florentine Codex. The players moved six pebbles round the board which was a mat with 52 squares. Beans were marked as dice. Each player tried to get three pebbles in a row to win the game. The Spanish writer Duran tells us how keen gamblers would carry their game mats around with them, and the dice tied up in small cloths.

Crafts and trades

Many Aztec commoners were craftworkers. Stone-workers, carpenters, potters, mat and basket makers, and weavers made everyday objects. Others were skilled in the more creative crafts — featherwork, metalwork, sculpting, jewellery-making, and painting. Aztec craftworkers learned their skills from descendants of the Toltecs. As a result, Aztec artists were known as the tolteca.

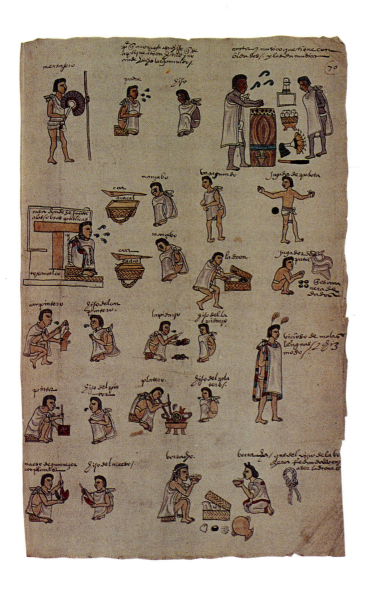

◁ **A featherworker.**
Featherwork was a skilled craft which took years to learn. The techniques were handed down from parents to children. First the pattern was designed. Then the children mixed the glues while the men prepared the cotton backing. The cotton was glued and reglued until it was stiff and shiny. The design was traced on to the cotton, which was stiffened with paper and maguey leaves. Meanwhile, the women prepared the feathers. The feathers came from colourful birds like quetzals, parrots and hummingbirds. Feathers from local birds were also used. They were dyed to the same bright colours as the more exotic feathers.

Most skilled craftworkers lived in the cities and worked from their own homes. A group of workers in the same craft often lived in the same **calpulli**. This meant that they were able to organize themselves into **guilds** and train **apprentices** to carry on the crafts.

Part of what we know about Aztec craftworkers comes from the **codices**. One picture shows a woman weaving on a **backstrap loom**. This type of loom is still used in Mexico today. One end is attached to the weaver by a strap around her waist. The other end is tied to a tree or post.

The Aztecs did not use much furniture but some houses had wooden chests and screens made by the carpenters. The Aztecs also made dug-out canoes and flat-bottomed boats, and carved drums and special masks for ceremonies and festivals. Potters did not use a wheel. They built up pots with strips of clay. Sculptors shaped statues by rubbing the stone with a piece of animal hide that had been roughened with sand. They carved the details with a copper knife.

Luxuries for the rich

Featherworkers, goldsmiths, silversmiths, jewellers and painters only worked for the nobility. They were highly thought of, particularly the metalworkers. They made gold and silver jewellery, body ornaments and ceremonial objects. The metals were melted in simple furnaces and moulded. The metalworker made a clay mould and covered it with a thin layer of beeswax and another layer of clay. The mould was heated so that the beeswax melted and flowed out through holes left in the clay. Then melted metal was poured into the space left by the wax. This method produced delicate and detailed work. One Spanish historian wrote '...they can make a piece half in gold and half in silver with all its scales, in gold and silver alternating'.

△ **This featherwork shield** is a good example of what the featherworkers produced. For a shield, the men glued the feathers on, finishing with a layer of brilliant colours. For clothing such as headdresses and capes, the feathers were sewn into the cloth.

△ **This turquoise ornament** would have been worn on the chest of a nobleman. It is made of gold and decorated with a stone called turquoise. Articles decorated in this way were made by lapidaries, craftworkers who worked with precious and semi-precious stones. They made necklaces, bracelets, earrings, pendants, lip plugs and other ornaments. They used stones such as amber, amethyst, jade and turquoise.

The market at Tlatelolco

The Aztecs produced so many goods that they needed markets in every village, town and city. Every household that grew food or made goods wanted to exchange what they had left over for other things they needed. Most markets were open five days a week. People went there to buy and sell, and to meet and talk to their friends. Travellers from all over the empire visited the big markets to buy luxury goods.

One of the biggest markets was in the city of Tlatelolco which was next to Tenochtitlan on the same island. The Spaniards were astonished when they saw it. The Spanish soldier Bernal Diaz wrote that huge crowds of people flocked around the stalls 'Some buying and others selling, so that the murmur and hum of their voices and the words they used could be heard more than a league (about five kilometres) off.' Another historian says that between 20 000 and 25 000 people came to the market every day, and between 40 000 and 50 000 came on the main market days.

Diaz also described the market and the goods for sale. He wrote about the dealers in gold, silver, and precious stones, feathers, cloaks, and embroidered goods, and male and female slaves who were also sold there. There were people selling **capes**, chocolate, sandals, deerskins, and food that included maize, beans, turkeys, young dogs and waterbirds. There was pottery, paper, medicines, salt and tobacco.

Buying and selling

The Aztecs did not have money so they bought and sold goods by **barter**. They exchanged their goods for other goods of the same value. There was a strict system for bartering. All goods, whether maize, gold, or a slave, were worth a certain amount of cocoa

◁ **The market at Tenochtitlan** probably looked like this reconstruction. The sellers spread their produce out on mats and sat on the ground, waiting for customers. People wandered up and down between the stalls, choosing fruit, vegetables, pottery and other goods. Each type of produce had its own special place. Vegetables were in one place, pottery was in another, and so on. There were no shops, so the Aztecs bought everything they needed from the markets, including chalk and limestone, candles and herbs. They also bought *chicle*. This is the juice from the tropical sapodilla tree and is the basis of chewing gum.

beans or cotton cloaks known as **quachtli**. One *quachtli* was worth between 65 and 300 cocoa beans. Gold dust was also used for bartering.

There were officials who made sure that the buyers and sellers did not cheat and charge prices that were too high.

Aztec prices
The Aztecs measured the price of something by how many cloaks (quachtli) or how many cocoa beans it was worth. The difference in value between cloaks and cocoa beans depended on the quality of both. The quachtli came in standard sizes. These are some prices when 1 cloak is worth 100 cocoa beans.

1 dug-out canoe = 1 cloak
1 slave = 25 cloaks
1 feather cape = 100 cloaks

Aztec merchants

Families who grew food or made everyday goods such as tools took them to market themselves. There was enough for the day-to-day needs of most people, including the nobility. The **merchants** or *pochteca* did not deal in goods of this kind. They were interested in the luxury items produced by the skilled craftworkers in the cities.

The craftworkers depended on the merchants for the materials they needed. Gold, silver, copper, lead and tin were mined in the mountains. **Obsidian** is a hard, shiny rock which stoneworkers made into mirrors, knives, razors and other tools. The rock had to come from the hills outside the cities. Feathers and precious stones had to be brought even greater distances.

The merchants travelled all over the empire and far beyond it, searching for materials to buy and bring back to the cities. They always carried valuable goods such as jewellery to trade. The Spanish priest Sahagun described the merchants carrying golden necklaces, obsidian razors with leather handles, needles for sewing, and shells. The merchants visited the markets to buy and sell luxury items. They were the ones who spread these goods throughout the empire.

The merchants formed a separate group of people

▽ **Aztec merchants.** This picture is from an Aztec codex. The merchants had their own god, Yacatecuhtli, who is shown on the left of the picture. He carries the sign of a cross-roads with footprints on it. A footprint is the glyph for a journey, so this is meant to show the travels of the merchants. Merchants themselves were shown carrying a fan and staff, like the merchant on the right of the codex picture. He has a load of quetzal feathers on his back.

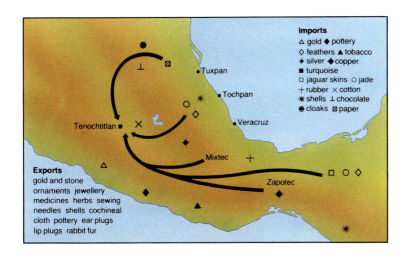

Imports
△ gold ◆ pottery
◇ feathers ▲ tobacco
✦ silver ◆ copper
■ turquoise
□ jaguar skins ○ jade
+ rubber × cotton
✳ shells ⊥ chocolate
● cloaks ⊠ paper

Tuxpan
Tochpan
Veracruz
Tenochtitlan
Mixtec
Zapotec

Exports
gold and stone
ornaments jewellery
medicines herbs sewing
needles shells cochineal
cloth pottery ear plugs
lip plugs rabbit fur

in between the nobility and the commoners. They had their own **guild** and their own law courts. They could own land and were allowed to send their children to the **calmecac** with the nobles' children. The government was in charge of all the trading and shared in the goods that the merchants brought back. Many of the nobles did not like the merchants because the merchants were so powerful. So the merchants were careful to dress in simple clothes and not show off their wealth in public.

Merchants travelled in groups with porters to carry the trading goods. They only set out on lucky days and timed their travels to return on a lucky day. (You can read more about lucky days on page 23.) Details of their trading were kept secret. They returned to the city at night in their canoes, and hid their goods away immediately.

The king's spies
Sahagun met merchants who had traded at Tlatelolco and they told him how the merchants acted as spies for the king. They often travelled through lands which the Aztecs had not conquered. They carried presents from their ruler to the rulers of these lands.

Travel and transport

The Aztecs never discovered that wheels could be used to move things about, so they did not have vehicles like carts. They did not have any pack animals such as donkeys either. Before the Spaniards arrived, people walked everywhere or went by canoe on the waterways. They piled produce from the **chinampas** into canoes and paddled them into Tenochtitlan.

The **caravans** of merchants travelled hundreds of kilometres in search of materials and goods. A line of porters would follow them, carrying goods for trading. The people who made up the caravan carried weapons, as the journey could be very dangerous. The merchants sometimes got mixed up in wars and had to be able to defend themselves. One story tells of a group of merchants who were captured and held prisoner for four years in a town near the Pacific coast. The Aztec king used this as an excuse to send an army to conquer the town. By the time the soldiers arrived, the merchants had already broken free and captured the town. Merchants never cut their hair on a journey. By the time they broke free, these merchants had hair down to their waists.

Difficult journeys

The merchants had to travel through many different types of countryside to find the materials and goods they needed. They passed through every type of climate. Tenochtitlan was in the middle of Mexico, in the mountains. Exotic feathers and precious stones came from the tropical lowlands along the Atlantic coast. Parts of the coast were very hot and dry, with burning sandy plains. Other parts were hot and damp, with tropical forests. To reach the tropics the merchants had to cross ranges of mountains with snow on the peaks.

The merchants and armies were the only people

△ **Merchants carried weapons** on their journeys, as this picture from the Codex Mendoza shows. Young merchants going out for the first time were lectured about the dangers and hardships they would meet along the way. When they returned, they were reminded to stay humble and to wear fine clothes and featherwork only in their own homes.

◁ **The volcano of Popacatapetl in Mexico.** This gives us an idea of how difficult it must have been for Aztec merchants to move their trading goods from one place to another. They would have had to go through this part of the country on their journeys from Tenochtitlan to the eastern coast.

who travelled long distances. Some of the nobility travelled between Tenochtitlan and their lands in the country. The commoners went to market and to their fields and perhaps into the cities to sell goods. They had flat-bottomed wooden boats as well as canoes.

◁ **Porters carried trading goods** for the merchants. Each man carried a load weighing between 20 kg and 30 kg on his back. This picture from the Codex Mendoza shows how porters carried loads using the Aztec strap method, with a rope passed round their foreheads and under the load.

Founding a city

Most of the Aztecs' early history is based on **legends**. Historians think that if their island home of Aztlan really existed, it was north-west of Tenochtitlan. In his history, Diego Duran says 'The rock is called Chicomoztoc...and from there came forth the Mexicans...and being thus very far-off, no one still knew later where it was.' Another historian worked out that the Aztecs had five new fire ceremonies between leaving their original home and settling down in Tenochtitlan. Ceremonies were every 52 years and the last of these was held in Tenochtitlan in 1351, so they must have left their island in about 1111.

◁ **The Aztecs' great journey** from their island home of Aztlan to their city of Tenochtitlan may have taken 200 years. They seem to have wandered aimlessly, sometimes getting lost 'in the mountains, the woods, and the place of the crags' as a note in a codex tells us. Some pictures show priests carrying the statue and feathers of Huitzilopochtli. The Aztecs built a temple to him wherever they stopped. Sometimes they fought other tribes. They took prisoners and sacrificed them to Huitzilopochtli.

The Hill of the Locust

The Valley of Mexico was already divided into city-states when the Aztecs arrived. The Aztecs tried to take farmland but their savage and aggressive behaviour made them unpopular. Wherever they went, people would drive them away. In 1299 they arrived at Chapultepec, 'The Hill of the Locust', near Lake Texcoco. They settled here but neighbouring tribes wanted to drive them out. The Aztecs chose Huitzilihuitl, 'Humming Bird Feather', to be their leader in the battles that followed. The other tribes won and drove the Aztecs away from Chapultepec in about 1319. The Aztecs **sacrificed** Huitzilihuitl and his daughter.

The Aztecs settle

The Aztecs fled to Culhuacan on the other side of the lake. The Culhua people who lived there banished them to a dry and desolate area thinking they would die there. In fact, the Aztecs did very well. They managed to combine farming with hunting and began to trade. Soon they wanted more power.

The Culhua's king, Culhuacan, asked the Aztecs to help them fight a neighbouring city-state. The Aztecs beat the enemy and then planned to attack the Culhua. They needed an excuse to wage war, so they arranged a marriage between their leader and Culhuacan's daughter, and immediately killed the girl. Fighting broke out and the Aztecs fled from Culhuacan to an island in the lake. Aztec legends say that the god Huitzilopochtli appeared to one of the priests and told him to search for a cactus with a great eagle perched on it. He said that he had named this place Tenochtitlan, 'The Place of the Fruit of the Prickly Pear Cactus'. The next day, the people found the cactus and the eagle with a serpent in its beak. They immediately built a temple to Huitzilopochtli.

△ **The founding of Tenochtitlan,** from the Codex Mendoza. In the centre is the cactus with the eagle perched on top. Around the cactus are ten Aztec leaders. The inside border, round the leaders, represents the lake. The lines across it show the four quarters of the city they were going to build. The glyphs at the bottom show Aztec warriors conquering Culhuacan and another city, Tenayuca, which they had fought against earlier in their travels. Around the outside is a border showing the 52 years of the calendar. At the bottom right is a new fire symbol, marking the start of a new 52 years.

Building an empire

The first Aztec ruler in Tenochtitlan was Tenoch. He wanted to make peace with Culhuacan, leader of the Culhua people. In 1372 the Aztec nobles decided to form an **alliance** with the Culhua. A Culhua named Acamapichtli was chosen as the new Aztec ruler and he came to live in Tenochtitlan.

This alliance gave the Aztecs more power but a tribe called the Tepaneca was still the strongest in the valley. Their leader, Tezozomoc, seized city-states and began to build an **empire**. He was a harsh ruler who demanded high **tributes**. The Aztecs suffered with everyone else until Tezozomoc realized that the Aztecs were good warriors. The Aztecs became allies of the Tepaneca.

The Aztecs gain power

For many years Tezozomoc tried to defeat the city of Texcoco which stood in his way of ruling the valley. He succeeded at last, took tributes from the city and gave them to the Aztecs. By the time Tezozomoc died in 1426, the Aztecs had a new ruler, Itzcoatl, who decided that the Aztecs should become warlike and aggressive again. The Aztecs decided to form an alliance with Texcoco and another city, Tlacopan. This gave them the strength to fight the Tepaneca. The Aztecs were the strongest members of the alliance. In 1428 the three cities waged war on the Tepaneca and captured their capital city.

The Empire grows

Itzcoatl died in 1440 and his nephew Montezuma I became king. He wanted to extend the empire by conquering lands outside the valley. His progress was halted in 1446 when Tenochtitlan was badly flooded and the king had the great embankment built. Then there were several years of bad harvests which led to a famine. Thousands of people died of

The Aztec rulers

Acamapichtli	(1372-1391)
Huitzilhuitl	(1391-1415)
Chimalpopoca	(1415-1426)
Itzcoatl	(1426-1440)
Montezuma I	(1440-1468)
Axayacatl	(1468-1481)
Tizoc	(1481-1486)
Ahuitzotl	(1486-1502)
Montezuma II	(1502-1520)

Itzcoatl

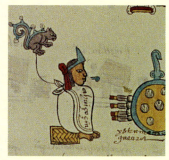
Ahuitzotl

Montezuma II

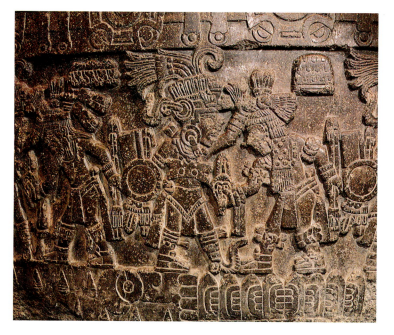

◁ **The Stone of Tizoc** is a carving showing the achievements of Tizoc, an Aztec king. He is grasping the hair of a prisoner. This was supposed to show victory. In fact, Tizoc was not a very successful ruler. He took over from his younger brother Axayacatl in 1481 but he only ruled for five years. During this time, the Aztecs were trying to conquer Metzitlan which was an independent city-state to the north of Tenochtitlan. They did not succeed and Metzitlan was still independent when the Spaniards arrived. Some historians think that the nobles killed Tizoc because he was not a good ruler. The nobles chose a strong general to rule after him.

starvation. Montezuma was determined that this would not happen again. He set out to conquer wealthy lands where there was good farmland. The Aztecs did not settle in these conquered lands. They allowed the lords of the lands to stay in control so long as they paid tributes to the Aztecs. Montezuma also continued to expand Tenochtitlan and fill it with impressive buildings such as the huge pyramid temple.

By the time Montezuma died in 1468, the Aztec empire was large and powerful. The next two rulers, Axayacatl and his brother, Tizoc, were not so successful. When Tizoc died in 1486, a general, Ahuitzotl, was chosen as ruler. He immediately waged war against rebellious states and took thousands of prisoners who were all killed in the temple. The king also wanted to extend the empire and conquered new lands along the Pacific coast.

When Ahuitzotl died in 1502, the nobles chose his nephew, Montezuma II, as the new ruler.

Aztec warriors

Every young Aztec boy knew that he would grow up to fight in wars. The Aztecs were ruthless warriors. Their skill at fighting allowed them to build up their huge empire. The Aztecs fought to make their people more powerful, and to make sure of tributes for the nobility. There was nearly always a war going on somewhere.

A successful warrior

All boys wanted to become warriors, whether they were **nobles** or **commoners**. Young boys were trained to fight and take prisoners. A brave and ruthless warrior was rewarded and could rise high in the army. An unsuccessful warrior was shown up in public. When a boy was ten years old, his hair was cut, leaving a lock of hair at the back of his neck. This lock was not cut off until the boy took his first prisoner. Sahagun writes that if a boy failed to take a prisoner he was known as 'big tuft of hair over the back of the head' and everyone else would make fun of him.

When a young man had taken his first prisoner he became an *iyac.* He was allowed to grow his hair so

◁ **Dressing for battle.** War lords and knights wore splendid uniforms covered with featherwork. The *ehuatl* was a featherwork tunic. The type and colour of the feathers showed the soldier's rank. For example, a captain wore red parrot feathers. The *tlahuiztli* was a complete featherwork garment worn by the highest-ranking knights. Feather headdresses also showed rank. All warriors wore decorations which showed which clan they came from.

that it fell over his right ear as a sign of his success. When he had captured or killed four prisoners he was allowed to wear special capes and attend the meetings where battles were planned. After that, he could become a *tlacateccatl* or commander. Rising to an important position in the army was a good way for commoners to become more important. They could become top commanders and receive a gift of land from the ruler.

The Aztec army
The best fighters became eagle knights who wore eagle's head helmets, or jaguar knights who wore jaguar skins in battle. Their uniforms showed their bravery and skill. They were full-time professional soldiers. Under them came thousands of ordinary warriors. All Aztec men except **slaves** had to do military service. They learned about war from the more experienced warriors.

When there was a war all the **calpullis** had to raise as many men as they could. They were organized into companies, groups containing between 200 and 400 men. The companies were grouped into larger regiments. Each regiment had a professional leader who was a full-time warrior.

The warriors fought with spears and **javelins,** pointed sticks that could be thrown a long distance. Some had wooden clubs edged with **obsidian**. They wore armour made of cotton which was padded to make it thicker and then soaked in salt water, or brine. This stiffened the material so that it could not be pierced so easily. The Spaniards copied the idea of cotton armour when they arrived because it was much cooler than metal. Warriors carried shields which were covered with hide and decorated with featherwork. The knights wore wooden helmets decorated with feather plumes.

△ **An** *atlatl* **or spear thrower.** Warriors hurled spears and javelins with these. The spear was slotted into a groove and held by a hook. A warrior could throw a spear at great speed with an *atlatl.*

Aztec warfare

Aztec rulers would start a fight for any reason. Their reason might be that someone had insulted them, or that a city had not paid its tributes, or that people from that city had attacked Aztec merchants.

The Aztecs did not launch a surprise attack. First they sent nobles from Tenochtitlan to the city they planned to attack. The nobles asked the city's leader to join the Triple Alliance. In return, the city had to pay **tribute** to the Aztecs, allow their merchants to trade, and put a statue of the Aztec god Huitzilopochtli in their temple. The city had 20 days to think about it. Then nobles from Texcoco arrived. They began to issue threats and warnings. Again, the leader had 20 days to consider the proposals. Lastly, nobles from Tlacopan arrived with gifts of weapons. The threats and warnings became more severe. If the city did not agree after another 20 days, the ruler sent messengers with gifts of shields, clubs or feathers. This meant that war had been declared. The long delay gave the Triple Alliance time to spy out the land and plan how to attack the city.

△ **Huitzilopochtli, the sun god and god of war,** wearing a headdress of quetzal feathers. Though the Aztecs enjoyed wars, the reason they gave for fighting was to please Huitzilopochtli. They took as many prisoners as possible, to sacrifice to the god. Every year, the wars began after the harvest had been gathered in. The people that the Aztecs attacked were terrified and treated the Aztec warriors like gods. They entertained and fed them. The Aztecs captured long lines of prisoners and took them away, with their hands tied behind their backs and their necks in wooden collars.

◁ **A prisoner being threatened by four jaguar knights.** He has a shield and weapon to defend himself. If he could defeat all four knights, the Aztecs would let him live. If not, he would be sacrificed.

Medicine and healing

An Aztec who was sick visited a **diviner** to find out what was wrong. The diviner threw maize seeds onto a mat. The Aztecs believed that the diviner could tell what the illness was by looking at the pattern the seeds fell in.

The next step was to see a doctor or **ticitl**. The Spanish historian, Sahagun, writes that a doctor was 'a knower of herbs, of stones, of trees, of roots... He provides health, restores people, provides them splints, sets bones for them...' Some ticitli went into war with the Aztec armies. They set broken bones and treated wounds with various mixtures including the juice from the maguey cactus.

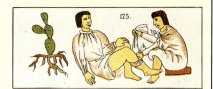

The ticitli used more than 130 herbs to make medicines. Mushrooms were used in many kinds of medicine, including medicines for fever. Patients were also given steam baths to sweat a fever out.

These two pictures from the Florentine Codex show someone taking medicine for fever, and the ticitl binding a broken leg.

Launching the attack

The leaders then got the army together. The warriors did not all come from Tenochtitlan. There were regiments from the three cities of the Triple Alliance, and also from the city-states that the Aztecs ruled. Priests foretold a lucky day to start the battle and many of them travelled with the army. Everyone carried food on their backs.

The battle was usually short and fierce. The aim was to take prisoners for sacrifice, not to kill people in battle. The conquering Aztecs burned temples and decided on what tributes the conquered city would have to pay. They made the conquered city show their respect for the Aztec leader and worship the god Huitzilopochtli. Then the Aztecs left with their prisoners. The Aztecs did not always win, however. Diego Duran writes about a battle they fought in 1478, when they lost 20 000 warriors from their army of 24 000.

Montezuma the king

By the time Montezuma II became ruler in 1502, Tenochtitlan was a huge city and most of its neighbouring cities were already part of the Aztec empire. Conquering new lands meant longer and longer journeys. The warriors complained but the leaders wanted more power and more tributes. The Aztecs needed more and more tributes to support their huge population. The priests urged the leaders to conquer new lands to keep the gods happy with blood offerings. The ruler Ahuitzotl had to pay money to the warriors to make them fight. When he died, the empire was at its most powerful, yet there was always danger of rebellion from those paying tribute.

△ **Montezuma wearing his royal robes.** A noble, on the right, puts on his headdress. The king is wearing a nose plug and ear plugs.

A new approach

Montezuma was a brave warrior. He was proud and often cruel, but he listened to his nobles who felt that the empire was getting too big. He decided not to extend it into new lands. Instead he tried to increase the power he held over neighbouring cities. There were still a few independent city-states in the Valley of Mexico. Montezuma concentrated on trying to take

◁ **This strange bird was one of the omens** or signs that meant something evil was about to happen. It was called an ashen bird and it had a crest on its head like a mirror. The Aztecs wrote that when some fishermen brought the bird to the king, he looked in the mirror and saw warriors riding on deer.

control of these city-states and bring them into the empire. The cities included the powerful city of Tlaxcala, and two other cities to the east of Tenochtitlan. Montezuma fought the Tlaxcalans from 1504 until 1519. He did not manage to conquer them.

Troubling events

The fighting was still going on when Montezuma was faced with new and frightening events. For several years before the Spaniards arrived, the Aztecs received **omens** that something evil was going to happen. We know about these from the Aztecs' own accounts, translated by Sahagun. All these accounts were given after the Spanish Conquest. The Aztecs may have been trying to give reasons for their defeat by the Spaniards. They talked about tongues of fire in the heavens. Lake Texcoco suddenly began to boil and destroyed houses on the islands. Lightning struck a temple, and a shrine in Tlatelolco suddenly burst into flames.

Then messengers brought tales of white men with beards who had landed on the east coast and were in Maya country. All the enemies that the Aztecs had fought before then were Mexicans. The Aztecs had no idea what lay across the sea and they were terrified. We only know what is supposed to have happened next from accounts given by Spaniards and Aztecs after the conquest. It is said that Montezuma remembered the legend about Quetzalcoatl, the Plumed Serpent God. Quetzalcoatl had vanished across the sea to the east, saying that he would return one day to claim his kingdom. Montezuma thought that the new arrivals must be gods and he prepared to welcome them in style. However, Cortes and his followers may have made up the story about Quetzalcoatl, since there is no other evidence for it.

△ **Montezuma in a procession.** The king is going to meet the leader of the Spanish expedition, Cortes. This picture was painted after the Spanish Conquest. It is interesting because it shows the Aztec king and his people as the Spaniards saw them. The Aztecs' clothes look far more elaborate than they do on the glyphs. Montezuma is being carried under a canopy. Behind him is an ornate litter which is carried on poles. In the background, Aztec commoners are following the procession along a canal in their canoes.

The Spanish conquistadores

In 1519 a Spanish fleet of 11 ships carrying 600 men landed at Veracruz on the east coast of Mexico. The Spaniards had been exploring South and Central America for several years before this. They had been searching for gold and any other valuable materials. It was reports of these earlier expeditions that reached Montezuma and filled him with fear.

During an expedition to the east coast of Mexico in 1518, the Spanish captain, Juan de Grijalva, had met a tax collector named Pinotl. Pinotl traded with the Spaniards and used sign language to tell them about an inland kingdom which was rich in gold. Grijalva reported back to Spain with this news and an expedition was organized. The commander was the soldier and explorer, Hernando Cortes.

Meanwhile Pinotl had hurried to Montezuma and told him about 'winged towers' (the Spanish ships) from across the sea. He said that white men with long beards would be coming to Tenochtitlan. It was then that Montezuma remembered the stories about the god Quetzalcoatl and began to make his preparations, He sents priests and warriors to meet the **conquistadores** at Veracruz. They carried precious gifts for the gods.

The Aztecs meet Cortes

The Aztecs paddled out to the Spanish ships in canoes. They thought that Cortes was Quetzalcoatl, and put on Cortes's head the snake mask decorated with feathers, that represented Quetzalcoatl. Cortes challenged them to fight but the terrified Aztecs paddled ashore and rushed back to Tenochtitlan.

Montezuma did not know what to do next. He sent more messengers to the coast, carrying gifts of gold. Cortes decided to visit Montezuma. On 16 August 1519 he set out with his small army to march to Tenochtitlan.

△ **A Spanish portrait of Hernando Cortes.** Cortes was 34 years old when he set off on his expedition to Mexico, so this portrait shows him as he would have looked then. He had been told to find out about the new lands and take them over for Spain. He had no orders to conquer the people. Cortes was obviously a great leader. His army consisted of soldiers, priests and craftworkers, and they all stayed loyal to him. He was also a ruthless man. When he met the Aztecs, he used their religious beliefs and lack of knowledge to destroy them.

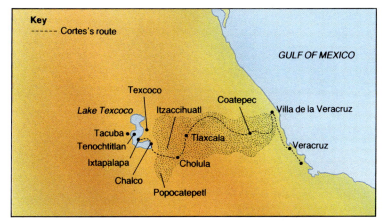

There are different stories about what Cortes was like as a man. Some historians say that he was a great general. Others say that he was cunning and greedy for gold. Whichever is true, he inspired great loyalty in his tiny army which set out across the dangerous, mountainous countryside to face the massive armies of the Aztecs.

Cortes was not challenged until he reached Tlaxcala, high in the mountains. Suddenly his army was surrounded by thousands of warriors. Cortes had horses and guns which the Tlaxcalans had never seen before. At first they were frightened and many of them fled. Then they came back to attack Cortes who was able to defeat them after bitter fighting.

Tlaxcalan leaders agreed to join forces with Cortes against the Aztecs. Montezuma heard from his messengers what was happening. Perhaps he thought that Quetzalcoatl was behaving in a very strange way and decided that the god must be angry with the Aztecs. It is more likely, though, that his messengers told him that the invaders were human beings, and not gods. Montezuma waited in fear for them to arrive. We know about the Spanish conquest of Mexico from Spanish historians and also from Sahagun's translation of the Aztecs' description of events.

△ **Montezuma's men met Cortes on board his ship.** When they gave him the gifts they had brought, Cortes fired a gun. The Aztecs had never heard gunfire before and they were terrified, as this picture from the Florentine Codex shows.

The fall of Tenochtitlan

T housands of Aztecs watched in bewilderment as the **conquistadores** approached Tenochtitlan. Sahagun described the scene as the lines of horsemen appeared, with swords flashing and the noise and smoke of gunfire. Cortes arrived on 8 November and Montezuma met him on a **causeway** outside the city. He welcomed the Spaniards like gods and took them back to his palace.

The Spaniards were amazed when they saw the riches of Tenochtitlan. Montezuma soon realized that they were only interested in gold. Cortes ordered that the statues of the gods should be destroyed and sacrifices should stop.

The Spanish behaviour showed Montezuma very clearly that they were not gods. He began to plot against Cortes. Montezuma had news of another Spanish fleet whose commander, Narvaez, planned to attack Cortes. Montezuma sent a message to Narvaez saying the Aztecs would help him. Then Montezuma told Cortes that new ships had arrived, and Cortes left for Veracruz to attack Narvaez. Cortes took Montezuma prisoner and left some of his conquistadores in charge of Tenochtitlan, under the leadership of a soldier named Alvarado. The king gave the Spaniards all the treasures in his palace, hoping that they would then leave. Instead, they melted down the gold.

The death of Montezuma

While Cortes was away, Aztec warriors gathered to celebrate the midsummer festival. Alvarado thought they were preparing to attack the Spaniards, so he ordered that hundreds of nobles should be killed. The angry Aztecs imprisoned the conquistadores in the palace. Montezuma tried to calm his people from the roof of his prison but he was killed. We do not know whether he was killed by the Spaniards or by

△ **Cortes speaking to Montezuma** with the help of Dona Marina, who is standing behind him. She could speak Nahuatl, the Aztecs' language, as well as Spanish, and translated what the two men were saying. She also advised Cortes in his dealings with the Aztecs.

△ **The Aztecs imprisoning the Spaniards** in the palace in 1520. At first the Aztecs prepared the beautifully decorated palace as a home for the people they thought were gods, and arranged feasts to entertain them. However, the Aztecs became suspicious of the way Cortes and his men were acting, and when Cortes took Montezuma prisoner, the Aztecs realized the Spaniards were not to be trusted.

THE FALL OF TENOCHTITLAN

◁ **The Spaniards conquer Mexico.** This painting shows some of the advantages Cortes had over the Aztecs. His army had weapons the Aztecs had never seen before, and strong metal armour and shields. Soldiers carried swords which could slice through the Aztecs' shields and wooden clubs. The army had heavy cannons and some of the soldiers rode on horses. The Aztecs' spears and arrows were no match for them. The Aztecs did not plan their battles but attacked in a solid mass. Cortes realized that if he killed the nobles, the commoners would lose heart without their leadership. By the time the Spaniards captured Tenochtitlan, all the houses had been pulled down and about 250 000 Aztecs had died.

the Aztecs who had lost faith in his leadership.

Meanwhile Cortes had returned to the city after defeating Narvaez. Many of Cortes's soldiers had been killed and on 10 July 1520 he was forced to lead his army away from the city. The Aztecs chose a new ruler, Cuauhtemoc. He tried to persuade former allies to help the Aztecs but he failed. Meanwhile, Cortes was getting support from cities who were pleased to see an end to the Aztecs' rule.

The leaders of Texcoco joined Cortes and this gave him a way in to the lake. He divided his army into three and fought his way up the causeways. He managed to get to the city and **blockade** it. The people could not get food and there was no fresh water. Thousands died. The blockade lasted for 93 days, then Cortes attacked again. His horsemen charged into the city and there was a last battle on the temple steps. The Spaniards finally captured the city in April 1521. Cuauhtemoc was taken prisoner and tortured. The Spaniards wanted his gold, not realizing that they had already taken all the Aztecs' gold from Montezuma.

New Spain

The Aztecs were defeated because they were fighting an enemy they did not understand. They fought wars to please the gods. They attacked in strength to take as many prisoners as possible. Their battles were usually over in a few days.

The Spaniards were used to wars which went on for many months. They planned each move carefully to make the best use of men and weapons. Cortes was not interested in taking prisoners, but in slowly making the enemy tired and unable to fight.

Ten years after the conquest, the whole of Mexico was under Spanish rule. It was renamed New Spain and Cortes became governor. The king of Spain sent word that the people were to be treated fairly, but Cortes only knew of one way to keep them under control. This was known as the *encomienda* system. A Spanish settler was given a group of Aztecs to work for him or pay him tribute. In return, he protected the workers and converted them to Christianity. In fact, the settlers made the Aztecs work *and* pay tributes. The Aztecs became little more than slaves.

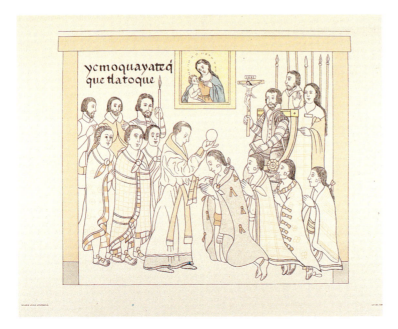

◁ **Aztecs receive Holy Communion,** part of a Christian service. After the Spanish conquest of Mexico, priests arrived in New Spain to teach the people about Christianity and convert them to the new faith. The priests learned Nahuatl and at first the people liked the religious ceremonies. In 1537 the Pope, Paul III, sent a message that no Christian should take away the freedom of the people living in Mexico. After this, the Spaniards no longer used the Aztecs as slaves, but they still believed that the Aztecs should be treated like children who needed the Spaniards to guide them. The Spaniards thought they were improving the lifestyle of the people by teaching them about religion, reading and writing, and the European way of working. In fact, they were destroying their culture.

◁ **The ruins of Montezuma's summer palace.** The Spaniards tore down Tenochtitlan. Everything was destroyed. All objects made of gold were melted. Cortes sent one or two pieces of featherwork back to Spain, and these have survived. The only other artefacts that were not destroyed were buried under the ruins of the city, and it is these that archaeologists are still finding. The Aztec social classes disappeared and most of the people became poor servants to the new masters. A few nobles survived but only because they were prepared to learn Spanish ways and live like Europeans.

Craftworkers were still needed but they were mainly the carpenters and potters who made everyday items. The goldsmiths and featherworkers no longer had anywhere to sell their work.

The Spaniards also brought diseases such as smallpox, measles and typhus. The Aztecs had no resistance to these and many died. In fact many more Aztecs died from diseases than because of deliberate cruelty by the Spaniards.

The legacy of the Aztecs

The Spaniards ruled in New Spain until 1821. The Aztecs were forced to give up their **calpulli** lands and many of their customs and religious beliefs. However, family ties remained strong. Today there are only about 3000 Aztecs in Mexico. They still speak Nahuatl, the Aztec language. If you go to Mexico today, you can still see some Aztec festivals, such as the yearly jaguar fights. These celebrations are Christian now, but the masks, costumes and dancing have their roots in the old Aztec ceremonies.

△ **The flag of Mexico** has the eagle and cactus symbol of Tenochtitlan in the centre. Other traces of the Aztecs survive, even though their civilization was destroyed nearly 500 years ago. Mexico City is a modern, Spanish-speaking city but only a short bus ride away some village people still speak Nahuatl and understand the Aztec calendar.

Time line

BC	
1300	Olmec civilization in Mexico.
AD	
300 – 900	Maya civilization in Yucatan.
900 – 1150	Toltec empire in Mexico.
1111	Possible date when Aztecs started their journey from Aztlan.
1299	Aztecs arrive at Chapultepec, 'The Hill of the Locust'.
1319	Aztecs driven away from Chapultepec. They flee to Culhuacan.
1325 (or 1345)	Aztecs found Tenochtitlan.
1372	Aztecs form an alliance with Culhuacan. Acamapichtli becomes king in Tenochtitlan.
1426	Tenochtitlan, Texcoco and Tlacopan form Triple Alliance.
1428	Triple Alliance overthrows the Tepaneca.
1440	Montezuma I becomes king.
1468	Death of Montezuma I. Axayacatl and then Tizoc rule empire.
1486	Death of Tizoc. Succeeded by Ahuitzotl.
1502	Montezuma II becomes king.
1504	Montezuma wages war on Tlaxcalans.
1518	Montezuma hears about white men in Mexico.
1519	Cortes's fleet lands at Veracruz. His army marches on Tenochtitlan.
1520	Cortes hears of treachery and returns to Veracruz, leaving Alvarado in charge. Alvarado orders massacre of nobles. Aztecs blockade Spaniards in palace. Montezuma killed.
1521	Fall of Tenochtitlan.
1531	The whole of Mexico comes under Spanish rule and becomes New Spain.
1821	End of Spanish rule in Mexico.

Pronunciation of Aztec words

Aztec word	Pronunciation
Acamapichtli	A-kama-pich-tlee
calipixque	kal-ip-isk
calpulli	kal-pulee
Chalchinuitlicue	Chal-chi-nooit-licoo
Chicomecoatl/Xilonen	Chiko-me-koatel/Shil-onen
chocolatl	choko-latel
Coatlicue	Koat-likoo
cuicalli	koo-i-kalee
Ehecatl-Quetzalcoatl	E-ekatel/Ket-sal-koatel
Huitzilopochtli	Wit-thil-o-poch-tlee
maguey	mag-oo-ay
Mayahuel	Maya-oo-el
Nahuatl	Na-wa-tel
Ometochtli	Ome-toch-tlee
patolli	pat-olee
pinole	pin-ole
pochteca	poch-teka
Popacatapetl	Popa-kata-petel
pulque	pul-k
quachtli	kach-tlee
Quetzalcoatl	Ket-sal-koatel
tamale	tam-ale
telpocticalli	tel-pokti-kalee
Tenochtitlan	Ten-och-tit-lan
Teotihuacan	Tai-ot-i-ooa-kan
teponaztli	te-pon-ath-tlee
Tetesinnan	Tet-es-innan
Tezcatlipoca	Teth-kat-li-poka
ticitl	tik-i-tel
tlachtli	tlach-tlee
Tlalacel	Tlal-a-kel
Tlaloc	Tlal-ok
tlapizcatzin	tla-pith-cat-thin
Tlatelolco	Tlat-el-ol-ko
tlatoani	tlat-oo-an-ee
tlatocan	tlat-o-kan
Tochtepec	Toch-te-pek
tonalpohualli	tonal-pok-ooal-ee
tortilla	tort-ee-ya
Xipe Totec	Shipe Totek
Xiuhtecutli	Sheoo-te-kutlee

Glossary

adobe: sun-baked mud bricks

alliance: a union or friendly agreement between two countries or states. They become allies

amatl: a type of paper made from bark

apprentice: a person who learns a craft or a trade by working for a skilled craftsman

aqueduct: a channel made by people for carrying water across a valley

archaeologist: a person who tries to work out what happened in the past by finding and studying old buildings and objects

architect: a person who designs buildings

artefact: an object that was made by people in the past

astrology: foretelling the future by studying the stars

atolli: a type of maize porridge eaten by the Aztecs

backstrap loom: a simple loom which is held tight by one strap around the weaver's waist and another strap tied to a tree or post

barter: to trade or bargain with goods

blockade: to surround a place so that the people are trapped inside with the aim of starving them or forcing them to give in

calmecac: an Aztec temple school for the sons of nobles

calpullec: an organized group of Aztec families who owned land that was farmed by the people. Each calpulli was run by a **calpulli** or headman

cannibalism: eating the flesh of your own kind

cape: a piece of cloth worn round the shoulders, like a short cloak

caravan: a group of merchants travelling together for safety

causeway: a raised roadway across water

chinampa: an Aztec floating garden

chocolatl: an Aztec word for a drink made from cocoa

city-state: a city that is also an independent state with its own rulers

civilization: a large group of people who have settled in one place and live in the same organized way. They follow the same customs and produce their own style in art

cochineal: an insect that lives on cactus plants in Mexico. It produces a bright red dye

codex: an Aztec book of picture symbols. The plural of codex is **codices**

commoner: a person who is not a noble

communal: shared equally between a group of people

compound: a walled or fenced area with buildings inside

conquistadores: Spanish conquerors

council: a group of people who are in charge of the day-to-day organization of a town or city

cremate: to burn a dead body

cuicalli: a school where Aztec children learned religious songs, dances and music

culture: the customs, thinking, art and general way of life of a group of people

diviner: a person who claims to be able to see the future by using magic

dowry: money given by a bride's father to a bridegroom on their marriage

dyke: (1) a drainage ditch (2) a high bank for holding back floodwater

embroidery: making pictures or patterns on cloth with coloured threads

empire: a group of countries or states ruled by one king or queen, who is often called an emperor or empress

excavate: to carefully dig up buried objects to find information about the past

fertile: describes rich soil where plants grow well

glyph: a picture symbol standing for a word or idea
guild: a society of people in the same trade

irrigation: watering crops by chanelling water from a river or lake along pipes or ditches

javelin: a type of spear

legend: a well-known story about the past, that is not always true
loin cloth: a cloth that covers the loins, the part of the body between the waist and thighs
loom: a piece of equipment that is used for making cloth

maguey: a type of cactus plant
matchmaker: someone who settled the marriage details between two people
merchant: a person who buys goods in one place and sells them somewhere else, often in a different country

noble: a person of high birth, such as a lord. The group of nobles in one country is called the **nobility**

obsidian: a dark shiny type of rock which comes from volcanoes
omen: an unusual happening or sign that some people believe means something is about to take place

patolli: a gambling dice game
peasant: a person who works the land for someone else
pinole: a type of Aztec porridge made from seeds

protein: an energy-giving substance found in foods such as meat, eggs and nuts
pulque: a drink made from maguey cactus

quachtli: a cotton cloak worn by Aztecs

sacrifice: to kill an animal or person as an offering to the gods
scribe: a person who wrote out documents and books by hand
sculptor: an artist who makes statues or other objects from stone or metals
shrine: an altar or small chapel to a god or saint
slave: a person who is owned by a master and has to work without pay
snuff: a kind of tobacco that is not smoked, but sniffed through the nose
solar: from the sun
soothsayer: a fortune-teller

tamale: a kind of maize pancake
telpocticalli: a school for the sons of Aztec commoners
ticitl: an Aztec doctor
tlachtli: a ball game played in ancient Mexico
tlapizcatzin: the caretaker of an Aztec temple
tlatoani: a ruler in Mexico before the Spaniards arrived
tonalpohualli: a type of Aztec calendar
tortilla: a flat bread made from maize flour
tribute: a type of tax paid in food and other goods

underworld: the place where the Aztecs believed people went when they died. The Aztec underworld had nine layers, ruled over by gods

vanilla: a type of orchid plant. The fruit of the plant is used for flavouring food

Index